Love on Fire

Maintaining the Passion in Your Relationship

Laverne Thomas

Copyright © 2015 Blissful Dream

Author: Laverne Thomas

All rights reserved.
ISBN-10: 0692578234
ISBN-13: 978-0692578230

LCCN: Pending

All rights reserved. No part of this book may be reproduced in any form or by any means without prior consent of the Publisher, excepting brief quotes used in reviews.

Cover by: Leigh Dan Drew for JahZoe Design Company

Typesetting/Editing/Self-publishing consultant:
Ty Waller for Young Dreams Publications –
www.youngdreamsbig.com

Love on Fire

Ways to maintain the passion in your relationship.

Table of Contents

Preface
Love..Page 1

Chapter One
Affection..Page 4

Chapter Two
Technology..Page 16

Chapter Three
Life Involvement...Page 23

Chapter Four
Reconciliation..Page 28

Chapter Five
Peace Within...Page 32

Conclusion
Fight..Page 36

What's next?
Poem...Page 38

About the
Author...Page 41

v

Preface

Love is a very tricky subject. It's something that we all want and/or may have fantasized about from a very young age. Some of the decisions we make as adults are sometimes based around the possibility of finding *The One*. Even as children, we are taught through fairytales that love is the ultimate goal in life. A charming prince has to find his princess in order to be complete. And after he finds her, everyone lives happily-ever-after. Sounds great, right? But what happens after we find that person? What do we do or say then to make things work? Who wouldn't want to have a shared life with that one special person?? We all do. However, the fairytales fail to show us the follow up cartoon of how the characters maintain their happily-ever-after.

No matter if you have found your love though traditional dating or online, this love is yours. It's exciting and mysterious in the beginning. There is frequent desire to be with that person, hear their voice and even touch them. But after a while, unintentionally, that changes. But, why? Various reasons can explain the changes every couple goes through. In a nutshell, *life happens*. Circumstances, lifestyles, environments and people change. We are human and change is definitely a part of life. The older we get, the more we grow and our needs change. So while life is happening and changing around us, what support is there to keep that love going strong for the long haul during these changes?

Just as fast as love can be found, it can be lost. Especially, if it is not respected or nurtured. To give you an example, I recently heard a story that compared a lover's relationship to the upkeep and maintenance of landscaping. At first I was skeptical in how the comparison would relate to love, but after thinking about it carefully, it made a lot of sense.

The story goes as such: "When you look across the street at your neighbor's yard, it is kept up very well. The grass is rich in color, bushes are nicely trimmed and even the flowers are blooming! Although gorgeous to look at, you get almost irritated by how lovely it looks. You think to yourself, *it only looks like that because they have all the time in the world to pay attention to their yard. I don't. I have to work and take care of what's going on inside my house.*

"And then you turn and look at your yard. There is nothing special about it that stands out to you. You don't cut your grass as often as you should, never really trimmed your bushes. Those flowers you planted a few months ago withered away because you didn't treat them properly. So it makes you wonder, if I had taken the time to nurture my yard the way my neighbor does theirs it would look just as good, or even better."

Well the same can be said for your relationship. If you are not seeing love's beauty in your relationship with your mate, it could very well be because you haven't taken care of it. Don't feel bad, many of us are guilty of this very thing. We get so comfortable being with someone that we forget to put in that extra work to keep things tight. We fail to think about the importance of love's labor until arguments and even divorce decrees are staring us in the face. If you want to keep your love burning over time, you have to remember to always put in the work. Depending on how much damage is done, you may even have to put in overtime. But for the one you really love, isn't the extra work worth it?

The next few chapters will give you tools that will definitely ignite that flame again - but it's up to you to keep it burning. These suggestions are great for new relationships and the older relationships that have some mileage. And for those that are still looking for love, these tools will prepare you for future love and hopefully stop you from making the same mistakes some of us already have. You can consider this as the "What Happens Next" portion of life that those cute fairytales didn't provide us. These tips have helped me reignite my marriage and hopefully it will help some of you do the same.

Chapter One

Affection

Affection is so important in the viability of a relationship. No matter if your relationship is new or long standing, the right display of affection will keep the connection between two people vibrant. Maintaining affection in your relationship can make a 20-year old love feel like that first week again. It's more than saying, "I love you" and having sexual relations. It's all about making the other person feel the love from you without ever saying a word. Now that's deep, but I promise you it's the best feeling ever. The connection between the two of you is supposed to be so strong that each of you has confidence in your soul that you are loved. It provides a wall of security that no one can penetrate.

So how do you do this? What is affection? Affection is not only in physical touch – affection is multifaceted, which I'll show you in a few steps ahead. The following expressions of affection are behaviors that I have personally experienced and I know they contribute to making love better (or can make love disappear with the lack thereof).

Conversation

Today, everything is completely about technology. We send our loved ones a text, tweet, Facebook message or email in place of having an actual conversation. Although these means of communication are fine and necessary at times, if constant, they will have you to miss out on core elements that emotionally connect you to another person. Communication is the foundation of every relationship, rather it be romantic, personal or professional. So in order for anything to work out with your mate, you have to learn how to effectively communicate.

Every so often, put down your devices and talk to your mate face-to-face. Actually sitting in front of the one you love and looking them in their eyes creates intimacy. Your expressions, tone of voice and body language shows the other person just how passionate you are about whatever you are discussing. Real conversation connects you on so many levels. It can link you two together spiritually, emotionally and even intellectually.

What am I supposed to talk about? Glad you asked! The conversation doesn't have to be deep or serious. Many people, especially men, shy away from real conversation because they are afraid of having the "feelings" talk. Nobody really wants to get too deep these days. Everyone is walking on eggshells, trying not to stir up a possible argument. But an intimate and meaningful conversation can be about anything. It can be about your day, what you ate for lunch, something crazy that happened at work, new happenings with the family or even something you saw online that made you feel or think a certain way. It really doesn't matter what the topic entails, it's really quite that simple- just start talking.

What will talking about my lunch do for my relationship? Glad you asked! Well, besides leaving the lines of communication open and free to talk about anything, it's creating an urge, a desire in you for more. The more you talk to your mate, the more your relationship will grow. You are going to want more mental stimulation with that person. When something happens or comes up during the day, you won't call your friends; you will call your mate. Why? Because over time, you have noticed that through the small conversations you've had, the other person genuinely expressed concern about you. Not that your friends are not concerned for you, but there is a different feeling of intimacy experienced when your mate is concerned about you.

They've learned your likes, wants, things that make you laugh and even things that make you cry. They've learned about you. And in their learning about you, it helped increase your love for them. You not only have a best friend, you have a best friend that you are in love with and that type of connection is the best to have. It creates a romantic bond that electrifies everything. It makes your conversations, activities together and sexual relationship better than you could have imagined. It creates a soul mate. The soul mate experience is created when you emotionally, spiritually and physically are connected to someone else. So do whatever you have to in order to experience that level of love. It's definitely something everyone should feel for themselves.

Compliments

Sweetie you look so pretty in that color! Baby that new hair cut is very sexy on you! Ooh, how we love to hear how our mates feel about us. Little sayings like these can make a huge impact on your mate. Letting your significant other know how good they looked or how much you like the way they did something was very frequent in the beginning. That's when you were impressed and wanted them to know they had your full attention. But over time, nice compliments are given less frequently or not given at all. Sharing honest compliments toward your mate is a good way to make them feel good and confident in the relationship. Flatter them and make them smile, doing these little things, like giving compliments, can have you on their mind all throughout the day. This is far better than them not thinking about you at all.

Everyone in a relationship wants to feel like they "still got it" or that your mate is still interested; genuine compliments do just that. Again, it promotes a healthy level of confidence for your mate (which is very vital in your love relationship), but also helps them know that you still see them as desirable. Knowing that you still find them attractive motivates them to continue doing all the little things you like. After all, when your mate goes shopping or to the salon, it is my opinion that 75% of what drives their decisions is based on what you like. So if you enjoy a certain style, haircut or even a specific way they walk through the room, don't be afraid to let them know it. It will make a world of difference in your relationship. My husband tells me all the time that he loves my natural hair with highlights. He hates when I wear weave. So although I enjoy a sew-in or braids, I'll wear my hair the way he likes it occasionally. So I don't stop doing what makes me happy, but I do a little of what makes him happy, too. This lets him know that I respect what he likes and want to make him smile anyway possible. And when he smiles, I smile! But I would never have the opportunity to do that for him if he didn't compliment me.

Never let your relationship get to a point when you stop complimenting your mate. Whether you believe it or not others compliment your mate regularly. However, your mate may have never actually noticed the compliments from others until they realized you were no longer doing it. No one should outdo you in complimenting your mate or giving them words of affirmation. When this happens the relationship danger zone could be quickly on its way. Your mate will no longer be concerned with trying to impress you, but rather concerned with impressing those who are actually paying attention to them. They are getting validation from someone other than the one they should. And although it can initially be innocent, things can turn into much more if not careful. So a good piece of advice would be to sweeten up your mate before someone else does.

Love On Fire

Physical

When I say *physical affection* I'm not talking about sex alone. I'm talking about making contact with another person. Physical affection is the act of letting your mate know that you want and love them without even saying the words. And there are so many simple things you can do throughout the day or week to do just that. So if at the end of the day sexual relations are what you really want, here are a few ways to ensure it happens. This advice is more catered toward the men because women are different when it comes to sex. Sex is an act for men, but it's emotionally driven for women. If a man does not do things to make a woman feel a certain way, she may not be able to perform. The lack of affection from our mates is the ultimate turn-off for women.

In the morning, before you leave the house, always give your mate a kiss. This starts the day off right, and if for some reason you don't see them again until later, at least you have made some sort of contact with them. While they are brushing their teeth, walk by and give them a peck on the cheek. Or if they are putting on their shoes, why not help them out with the last one by grabbing their legs. Help them button their shirt or touch their face while they are brushing their hair. Look at something small being the bigger picture. All you need to do is make contact and emotions will take it from there.

Later on that day while they are cooking dinner, a quick neck kiss can set quite the fire. Try grabbing their waist with a quick bottom rub. Something about the touch of the waist –especially for a woman- just screams intimacy alone. Any quick and play touch can seem sensual and get things started for later. If they are reading or doing a little work on the computer, stop and kiss an ear and walk away. I guarantee you they will remember that you paid them a little attention while they were working when they return to bed later. See them in the hallway and give a smack on the bottom, followed by some serious eye contact, this is as innocent, yet as sexy, as it gets.

For a couple living together or with children, a good way to create intimacy is interrupt their routine by picking up their responsibilities. Unexpectedly cook, clean or pick up the children so that your mate can rest. Take out the garbage, take the cars to get oil changes, whatever it may be that your mate does regularly for you. Do it for them and it will pay off. Your mate will be so appreciative and turned on by your generosity, all at the same time – this is especially true for women. Women wear so many hats and do so many things for other people throughout every day that they can feel like no one does anything for them. Many times when women feel that no one does anything for them, they are really referring to their mates. Giving the kids a bath and putting them to sleep so your mate doesn't have to will make all the difference. In the woman's case, she will have more energy to use on you later! Don't believe me, try it! My husband caught on and cooks dinner at least once a week so I don't have to. He learned fast!

These are just a few little things that can be done to show a little affection throughout the day. You know your mate better than anyone. You know what light touches turn them on or makes them giggle. Tap back into the shameless flirting you did in the beginning of your relationship. Never lose sight of that. And if you do, snap out of it and give these things a try. Your main goal should always be contact. Always make some sort of physical contact with your mate every day. As infants, we loved physical contact with our parents. It was our first signs of love and protection. It's undoubtedly the same needed feeling as adults. Your bodies need to feel comfort with each other daily - it will pay off later on in the evening.

Communication

Have you ever heard the statement, "It's not what you say but how you say it?" Of course you have. And do you know that it is a very true statement? No matter the setting of the conversation, professional or personal, properly communicating your topic of choice is key to building a relationship with another person.

When speaking to someone you are in a relationship with, your tone, body language and verbiage used is very important. It not only sets the temperature of your environment, but it allows others to *hear* how you feel – not *see* how you feel. If you are yelling, cursing and using large hand gestures it tells me you are very angry. When someone is really angry, the best thing the other party can do is not respond to him or her. So if you want a response back for active communication, please calm down first. I am not suggesting that you have to be a saint and never get mad; however, the old saying is true: *if you want more sweetness, use honey not vinegar.*

Example, if your significant other did something you didn't like you could respond this way, "Why the *fuck* did you do that?" Just those words alone lets me know you are upset about something, add in a loud tone and hand gestures, and now I'm beginning to feel the need to protect myself against your harsh words and tone. Naturally, I will have a feeling to respond, that response can be calm or it can be just as lethal as your initial question. My inner instincts and defenses kick in strong and now we're having a full on verbal fight. And in most cases, this type of argument leads to physical violence on both parts. So to avoid getting to that level, try speaking to each other differently.

How do I do that when I'm truly upset about something? Take that same question and rephrase it, try, "Babe, why did you do that?" It is the same question, looking for the same answer, but stated in a much friendlier manner. Hearing that, I know you are bothered by something I did and want to know why. If your tone is normal and you're, maybe, touching my hand I immediately feel your genuine need of my response. I don't feel scared or intimated. I don't feel a need to fight fire with fire. I immediately feel comfortable and ready to engage in an actual conversation. You created a calm atmosphere that allowed me to give you honest communication. People are more likely to speak freely and

Love On Fire

honestly when they feel the climate is calm. A volatile climate will generate the total opposite response.

Sounds super simple doesn't it? But surprisingly many people usually start their communication with the first scenario far more than the second. Although every situation differs and every person does as well, the goal is the same. You want an honest and sincere response. However, you will never get the response you're seeking by starting your communication in a negative way. Fiery conversations are not conversations at all. Instead it's a word match - two individuals yelling and screaming words with no meaning, which can have a negative effect on your relationship.

As children we are taught, *sticks and stones can break my bones, but words will never hurt me.* That's a bunch of bull. Words can and do hurt people. Especially the ones you love. You have to always remember that once you say something hurtful, demeaning or just plain cruel, you cannot erase it. Those words you spoke and the consequences of those words can haunt you even years later. If the offended person thinks about the situation, they can begin to feel that hurt as if it just happened. Some people may never get over things said if the words spoken were very painful and left an emotional scar on their hearts. Their minds will take them back to that same place every time an emotional sensor is triggered. So if you want your mate to always reminisce and have good emotions about you, watch what you say.

This is why my husband and I are working on not texting each other when we are mad. The words you type can be so nasty when you are mad. After an argument, especially if it has not been resolved, we try to stay away from messaging one another. We have a very good reason for making this rule. When he says something hurtful to me via text, reading it seems even more painful to me than if he had said it out loud. It's more hurtful for me because I feel he had an opportunity to erase the text before he sent it… and he didn't. So if I cried from that initial text, even if we reconcile later, if I read that text again my feelings are hurt all over. This is why, now, if we do have a heated texting match, I'll delete his messages the same day so I can't go back and read them again later.

My husband seems to love when I send him mean texts. He has a habit of sending screen-shots of those not-so-nice messages I have sent him when he wants to prove a point later. He uses it as ammunition against me. He throws them in there when I'm not expecting them. When I read them, I say "Why the hell does he still have this?" So now I watch what I say and how I say it to him. Those messages can really work against me when I'm winning in an argument! And since I love to win, I had to change things up a bit.

There is a difference between talking to someone and talking at him or her. Talking to someone is when you're actively involved in the conversation. You talk, they listen, they talk, and you listen. You're on equal grounds and more information gets through on both ends. Now, talking at someone is very different. This is when you speak with no regards for the other person. You don't care what they might say back, how they feel or even if they understand you. Your only agenda is to get your point across without receiving any feedback, good or bad. You can come off very dominant when talking at someone. This makes your mate feel small inside. When you're being dominant in a conversation or even in an argument with your mate, you can make them feel like they are having a parent/child interaction, this can be a very dangerous area in a relationship.

Making your mate feel like a child or subordinate is not only wrong, but also unfair. If two adults are in a relationship, they both need to be treated the same. There is no mother or father in a romantic situation. So there is no need for one to feel less than the other. If you are belittled often and treated with no respect, stop reading this book and create your exit plan. That relationship is toxic and unbalanced and you need to leave.

Being able to effectively communicate is the most essential element to any relationship. We have to be able to articulate our needs, wants, desires and dislikes. We need to have a voice and feel safe to express it. We have to also be able to listen and have compassion for what our mates are saying. We have to learn what they want and need as well. If you have someone in your life right now that is genuinely interested in what you have to say daily and is able to respond in a positive manner, you might have *The One* – you two could conquer the world. If the both of you can have a real conversation about the small stuff, your foundation is built tough enough to handle the big stuff life has to offer. And life doesn't hold back for anyone, so you have to be ready. With the right one, you are prepared for battle.

Chapter Two

Technology

I know you are probably thinking, "What does technology have to do with my relationship?" Well, seeing that it is currently 2015, this topic has become very popular among couples within the last few years. This is because we use so many different forms of technology to communicate. Rather it is through text or social media, spaces of technology is where we express our thoughts, desires and feelings. So if the use of one of these various forms of communication is not used in support to and for the benefit of nurturing your relationship, things can go bad quickly.

Cell Phone
Our cell phones are our absolute best companions now. We do everything with our phones. We make calls, search the web, engage in social media and can have conversations with literally anyone, anywhere. And now with so many security apps, our

phones also hold some pretty private information, which is why handling our cell phones with our mate is so important.

When you are on your phone constantly it sends a signal to your mate. It gives the perception to your mate that something or someone has your attention more than them. When you are with your mate your phone should not be of priority. Your mate should hold your amusement, entertainment and conversation. I mean that is the reason you are with them anyway, right? If real time with your mate can't replace your activities on your phone, this can be a very clear indicator that maybe you are not with the right person or your relationship may need a tune-up. Trust that your mate feels the same way by your obvious neglect and lack of attention.

Don't be the one taking your cell phone all over the house with you because you are afraid to put it down. That immediately shows that you don't trust your mate and they probably shouldn't trust you. Unless you have children, have an ill parent that doesn't live with you, or some other extenuating circumstances that forces you to have your phone connected to the hip at all times, put the phone down. Especially when you are entertaining your mate, they need to feel they are first priority. It would be a shame to lose your mate to your Smartphone!

My hubby loves watching videos of practical jokes. Although I understand and love to hear his laugh, it bothers me when he is on the phone too much. When his video watching has more attention than me it hurts. I feel ignored or boring. Why doesn't he just talk to me or watch a video with me is what I ask myself. It might seem silly to you, but for the other person it can be hurtful. There is only so much time in the day, so spend it in the real world with people who love you and not in the cyber world where no one even knows you.

Now you are probably saying, what about my privacy? My cell phone is my business. Privacy is important for everyone to have and respect. We should be able to keep some things to ourselves and only share if wanted. But in a committed and serious relationship your cell phone should not be one of those things. Your mate should be able to answer your phone or even make a phone call without worrying about lock codes. You should never feel uncomfortable or scared to pick up your mate's phone. You have to make your mate feel secure in knowing that there is nothing in there that they should not see.

Don't get the wrong idea. In no way should your mate be snooping through your phone searching for things that may or may not be there. But rather you are hiding something or not, passwords gives off the impression that you are not being honest. It simply says that either you don't trust them or they shouldn't trust you. Allowing your mate access to your device whenever creates a since of comfort in knowing that you have nothing to hide. And most times than not, if that feeling of trust is there, they won't even have the desire to go through your phone. That initial thought is created when you make the phone completely off limits.

For example, when I asked some friends about snooping in their man's phone I was given some interesting responses. When they date a man that leaves their phone around them, whom doesn't have it in their hand at all times and actually leaves the ringer on, they say they never have a desire to touch it. They feel as if the guy is not hiding anything and doesn't create suspension. But for the ones that their mate turns their ringer off, walks in every room with the phone, has a passcode or lock on their phone at all times, these women says it makes them crazy. It always sends the sign that he is not being honest or faithful. There are the times these women may even try to answer their phone or look through messages. Although it may not be right, the reason for doubt was clearly set by sneaky behavior.

Social Media

I believe at one point in time, we all have experienced a social media battle with our significant others. It seems absolutely insane to think about initially but social media today plays a huge role in relationships. Why? Right now, social media is the strongest form of public affection. Everyone in the world can see you declare your love with a simple picture or status update. You can even tag the person and visually let the world know you are in a relationship with another person on the Internet. So how could we not understand how important this concept has become?

Establishing your relationship on social media may not be important to some, but to many it's everything. Not letting the world know who that special person in your life is can seem very suspicious. It can come off as if you are hiding your mate from the world; especially if you are a big social media user who is constantly uploading all of your life's moments. Sharing pictures and updates of your friends but not of your mate says quite a profound message. There are different levels to the social world and your mate. Just like our relationships transition from one phase to the next, so do our levels on social media.

Will you be my friend?

Do you allow the person you are dating be your friend on social media? Now that's a tricky question. If you add your mate, you have officially opened your life up to them. Everything you think, say and do can now be monitored. If you are a committed person doing no wrong this won't be a problem for you at all. But if you are not an honest person in your relationship, this will literally open Pandora's box. And if you don't friend your mate, that can open an entirely different box- a box full of suspicion, distrust and arguments.

Unless you both have come up with an agreement to not involve social media in your relationship for privacy reasons and avoidance of conflict, there should be no reason your mate cannot be your friend. This simple connection allows each other access to your virtual life. This can create safety and security within your relationship. And those two feelings alone will continue to let your mate know you love and trust them.

Status Update

Once your relationship progresses and a relationship title is established, don't hide that from everyone. Announcing your affection publicly for one another not only lets each other know this is official, but others as well. Side note: This may be a good time to delete ex-partners from your page. Possible negative comments from ex-lovers can cause quite a debate with your current one. When you don't show who you are in a relationship with it appears as if you are still available. Even if that's not your intention, there are more predators online than in real life. So trust that they are watching your every move waiting to send you an indecent message or status. And this will cause ill-feelings from your mate that can damage your relationship. A great way to let your mate know you love them is by announcing it to the world with no regrets.

"Selfie Time"

People happy and in love take lots of pictures. Why? Because capturing the memory with a picture allows them to not forget those great moments when they felt the best. Moments together when they felt that undeniable love for each other. If you want to make your baby feel all warm on the inside, upload a few pictures with cute captions. I personally know women love to see that their mate has added a cute couple picture. The random times my husband posted a picture of me saying, "My beautiful wife," made me blush for hours - especially since he is big on privacy on social media. So a little thing like that made me feel loved. Things like that not only make us smile on the inside, but feel good knowing our mates are not hiding anything. You should want everyone to know that your mate is the reason you are having a great time. Not just today, but every day. So take a few pictures with your sweetie and let the world know you are in love.

This is not to be done for everyone that you date. Taking pictures with a few different people all the time shows inconsistency and instability in your life. Try to refrain from sharing your virtual life with everyone you date, but instead save it for the ones you love.

Chapter Three

Life Involvement

When you love someone and want him or her to know it, share your world with him or her. What does this mean exactly? It means that you no longer operate as an individual but as a team. Invite them to family gatherings or just spending time out with friends. You can even bring them along to do some of your daily or weekend routines. Including your mate in various areas of your life will ultimately create a greater bond. It will also provide a sense of safety and security. These are two big things that love and emotion thrive from. This is key, especially for married or engaged couples. Once married, two becomes one. It does not mean you have to give up your own individuality; but you are meaningfully sharing your life in all areas with your mate.

Family
Your family loves you and wants only the best for you. So if you feel your mate is the best, why not bring them around your family?

Love On Fire

This is a great way to keep the fire going in a relationship. Why? Because nothing says I love you more than trusting me to be around other people you love and that love you. This creates a sense of security because your partner knows that you consider them family, too. This can also have a positive effect on you as well because your loved ones will get to know and, hopefully, embrace your mate. If not, a lack of family involvement and acceptance can cause a great rift in your relationship. If that's your problem, that's a whole other book to read. Just be cautious, because if your family and friends are not *vibing* with your mate it can usually be a sign that something is off. They know you more than anyone, so if they sense something negative or not cohesive with your relationship it may be worth looking into. Sometimes outsiders can see what you don't while you are floating in a love fog.

It's not just enough to have your mate around your family, but spend time with theirs as well. Let your loved one know that their family is just as important to you as your own. This is especially important for married couples. Once you become one, your oneness includes each other's families as well. Take time to talk to their friends and family members when you get the opportunity. Just try not to share business about your relationship. Sometimes giving information about your mate can cause more harm than good. Loved ones are great, but serve a better purpose as supporters and not counselors.

Although you should stay away from getting into deep conversations about your relationship with friends and family, you should say a few compliments about them. This is a great opportunity to grab some brownie points with family members, which can pay off at times you wouldn't expect. Don't be afraid to set boundaries with your family. Create safety for your spouse by letting others know there is a limit to how far they can go with your mate. This ensures that no one intentionally, or unintentionally, crosses the line with him or her. Family is important, but not at the expense of your mate.

Friends

You are the company you keep. In saying that, your friends say a lot about you. You more than likely share common interest and experiences. They know your likes and dislikes; they know if you are just playing around or are truly in love. When you share your friends with your mate, it makes that connection stronger because you have added them into your real world. Your time with your friends is where you feel the most comfortable and actually where you want to be most of the time, outside of being with your mate. Including a mate in that experience periodically, not only secures the bond, but also strengthens the friendship between you both. It lets them know that you see them as important and want them around as often as possible.

When your mate doesn't know or have never met your friends this can be a sign that maybe you don't love this person the way that you may think. And not wanting to meet theirs, says the same. Not including that special person in your social life can come across very hurtful to your mate. You may think that they don't notice, but they are definitely paying attention. And the topic will eventually come up, whether you are prepared or not. So save yourself the argument, decide if your mate is the one you want to be with long term. If they are, bring them around the crew. If they are not, make sure you are being honest in informing them that you are casually dating - and casual dates don't meet the family. It causes confusion and unnecessary introductions.

Hobbies

Everyone needs his or her alone time. This is especially true when you are in a relationship. You need to maintain you regardless of the level of your relationship. But there are ways to make your partner feel special by sharing some of your most favorite things with them. Hobbies or fun routines are a great place to incorporate a loved one or someone you are trying to get to know better. It's fun sharing things that you find relaxing and exciting with your mate. It's even better when you create new hobbies together that you can call your own. The more time spent enjoying each other's company, the stronger the love will become. Allowing your mate into your world will let you know if this is the one forever or the one for right now.

For instance, my husband loves football. I don't. It's not like I hate it, but I would rather be getting my hair and nails done during that three-hour time span. Sometimes I feel he probably loves everything about the game more than me - and because of that, it makes me dislike it even more. It occupies all of his time and energy. But because I love him, I've tried to enjoy the sport with him in various ways. I attend a few of his games that he coaches. I will go shopping for his favorite team's apparel for him and the entire family to wear. And I've attended one professional game with him, but realized I held him back from truly enjoying the experience. So as his loving wife, I purchased the next set of NFL tickets for him and his best friend to enjoy. This way we shared something, I supported his interest and I realized where I needed to allow him to enjoy something on his own.

Chapter Four

Reconciliation

We learn as children how to apologize. So why is it so hard for us to do as adults? And why is it even harder for us when we're in relationships? Why? Righting your wrong is so vital to maintaining your relationship. When you've hurt someone, you must also be sure to aid in healing that person. Don't just let them deal with the pain? Own your part and say I'm sorry. Some people believe that just saying the words won't change anything. That's only true for those that might be apologizing for the same thing repeatedly. But if you've done or said something wrong and understand why it hurt the other person, apologize. Sometimes, acknowledging to your mate that you authentically understand how what you've done hurt them can help make their forgiving you easier.

It is absolutely imperative that your apology be genuine. Don't say it just to smooth things over. Apologize because you've recognized the mistake made and want your loved one to forgive you and feel better. A meaningless apology is worse than never saying it at all. It gives a perception that you are not taking your mate's hurt seriously; that can cause severe damage in your relationship.

If you don't know exactly what to say the next best thing is a touch. Allow the other person to feel how sorry you are. This can be with a strong hug and hold followed with a kiss. The sincerity should be felt from you to the other person. When it's real, your partner will feel it and eventually begin to let their guards down; once their guards are down the healing for them can begin. You may even see them shed a tear, especially for the woman. We underestimate the power of the human touch between two people that love each other. That natural electricity can make a bad day better instantly. So if you're unable to say the words, let your partner feel your sincerity. There is no telling where this kind of apology will end up!

Never ever just let things go. Ignoring current issues in a relationship can destroy it later. If you have an argument, whether serious or petty, address it. Never sweep anything under the rug. The more issues you push under the rug, the higher the pile becomes and eventually you won't be able to walk over it anymore. Those same issues will still remain on the inside of your partner. When issues are internalized and the other person is left dealing with them on their own, it's wrong. That mate becomes either very sensitive or very hard. It all depends on how they handle things. Those issues become bruises, hurting even more every time another issue gets piled on.

And what happens to the wounded soldier? Being captured by hurt makes your mate unable to be them. Over time they no longer have the ability to be happy because they will be full of resentment, anger and frustration. No one wants to be around a person who is full of all that. Prevent your mate's nasty character from making a debut role in your life movie by simply apologizing.

And never apologize through a text message. Apologize the same way you hurt your mate, in person. All the yelling and screaming didn't come though text, it was done in person. So own the pain you've caused and stand in front of your mate and apologize. Never hide behind something you've done. Stand in front of it. It will make the reconnecting and reconciliation much better between you and your mate.

When you love someone, never be afraid to admit when you're wrong. There is no harm in that. No one is taking score. There doesn't have to be a winner or loser. Just be willing to humble yourself enough to ease the pain of someone else. And you will realize that your willingness to reconcile will encourage your partner to do the same when it's their time.

Apologizing drops the guard of your partner and allows love to flow again. Once that happens, making up can happen naturally. Making up after a fight is exciting, if done correctly. It can be full of passion and bring the both of you closer together. When you can get through a hard time and reconcile properly your security as a couple builds. Don't miss that opportunity to make things better. Don't let the inability to apologize be the reason you lose your sweetie.

Chapter Five

Peace Within

Believe it or not, the ultimate key to a happy relationship is for you to be happy with yourself. It's very easy to lose yourself in a relationship because the love takes over. You forget about you and want to make the other person happy. You want to nourish their needs and supply their wants. There is nothing wrong with that at all as long as you don't forget about yourself.

You have to remember that your individuality and style is what attracted your mate to you. You, in your element, doing things that made you happy shined through you to them- it was without effort. You were living life and doing what made you whole. Maintaining your wholeness in your relationship is very important. You have to take care of you in order to effectively take care of someone else. If you don't, here are a few things that will happen.

Frustration, Resentment and Separation

If you put all of your energy into your mate and forget about you, you can end up very unhappy. Your mate, especially men, will continue their same routines. Their lives won't change much except now they have you in it to make things better. Their professional and social life will remain the same. However, this has become very frustrating for you. You may begin to feel that your mate is not as attentive to you as you are to them - especially when there is a marriage or children involved.

You now become the parent and spouse forgetting to take care of your needs. This new role brings on a new routine. If you neglect yourself completely for the spouse and parent routine, negative feelings will start to develop. These negative feelings will start to manifest in ways you won't even imagine. You no longer say sweet things to your mate. Instead of wanting to spend time nourishing the relationship with the little things you used to do, you now feel like you're performing meaningless chores in your relationship that you no longer want to do.

Love On Fire

A way to prevent this from happening is to remember you. Remember that before you were in a relationship all you had was you. After that relationship ends, all that will be left is you. In order to get through the good and tough times in your relationship, you have to nourish you at all times. Remember that before them (your mate) you had dreams and desires that were never meant to stop because you found love. If anything, that new love is supposed to encourage and increase those desires. You now have a teammate that is supposed to add value to your vision and not subtract from it.

If you start feeling uncomfortable and unhappy; if you start feeling irritated and angry all the time because you feel they don't appreciate your sacrifice; if you start feeling inferior in your relationship, brace yourself because the pain is coming next. You will begin to look at your partner differently. It's not because they did anything specific to you, it will be because you did something to you. Your unhappiness within yourself will start to seep out in petty arguments. You will now have an attitude when they leave the house to do a regular routine and you remain home taking care of business. All of the little things will become big, magnifying every issue that comes up.

This type of tension can seriously damage a relationship, or even end it. If you want to hold on to your mate, hold on to yourself. You can do this by doing the simple things that make you happy. It can be small things like working out, shopping, reading or attending church. Don't lose your friends. Keep a social life. It may not be as busy as it was when you were single, but keep it alive. Getting away from your mate is good not only for you, but for your relationship. Don't stop working. If you are a parent now and want to stay home with the kids, that's great. Just make sure you are doing something additional that makes you happy, besides just raising the little ones. They need to see that desire and drive in you as well. It's not only a turn on for your mate, but motivation for your entire family.

Some things will naturally change once you become in a more serious relationship. One party may be more indifferent in the relationship than the other. That's alright as long as it is discussed in a healthy way and both parties have a mutual understanding. Couples should communicate about all things expected and unexpected with their relationships. Especially when transitioning from dating, to living together, to married and now family. Shifting from one phase of a relationship can be exciting but difficult at the same time. Take time out to discuss how things should be before they get out of hand fast. You don't want all those negative feelings to stay bottled up and cause your relationship to end. Talk about it and work through it together. If it's worth fighting for, it's worth figuring it out.

Conclusion

Fight

The things discussed in this book are meant to help you keep that fire burning in your relationship. Maintaining a healthy and balanced relationship is very hard work, but it's worth it when it's for the right one. Nothing worth having is easy. You have to roll up your sleeves and put in hard time in order to see the fruits of your labor. Giving your all to a relationship should be effortless for the perfect person. At times, it will feel almost like second nature. But occasionally giving your all may not feel as effortless; you might have to be reminded of the little things you may have forgotten along the way to transition back to a smoother time in your relationship.

Love is great to have but can be difficult to hold on to at times. As long as you have love in your relationship and a willing participant, you will always have the opportunity to make your relationship work. Both people must be ready. After all, a boxer can't get in the ring and fight alone. The other fighter must be there, too, ready to meet you in the middle. When things seem a little dim in your relationship, grab your teammate and get to work. As long as you have someone willing to try, you have a chance to make things better than before. You have a chance to keep the fire burning forever.

Just remember to communicate your needs and wants. You have to notice the signs before things get bad. After all, you don't get off at the exit on the highway without using your turning signal. So use the same concept with your relationship. Work on things before they get so out of hand and someone gets off the highway. With that being said, try to use the concepts discussed throughout this book to hold on to the love you created. Work through the hard times and enjoy more of the good ones. Because when it's good, love is amazing. So allow yourself to enjoy that great feeling with the one you can't live without. Otherwise, what's the point of it all?

What's Next?

I love writing. My writing started with poems. I would write when I'm sad, happy or just confused. So I am currently working on a poetry book. Hopefully through my heart and art, I can encourage more people to do what makes them happy. As a bonus to this book, I'm attaching a sample of a poem that I wrote while finding my peace of mind last year, which led to me writing this book. Hope you enjoy it and let me know what you think…

Pain Brings Peace
When you cry, and you cry and you cry
But you can't figure out where it hurts
All you know is that it's tender and sore
And hope it gets better before it gets worst

When your pain feels physical
But the source is emotional
and you feel like you are losing control

Love On Fire

But you seem to can't let it go

Closing your eyes is the only freedom
Darkness and silence is your peace
Opening your eyes seem so hard to do
Cause it's the gate that will quickly release

Every tear, scream, cry out for more
For something better than you ever had before
For happiness, some joy, to simply enjoy sunshine
For love, sweet peace and for bliss that is all mine

So what do you do, when this pain comes upon you
How do you move when you have nowhere to go
Trust there's more, hope it's greater
Stand on expectation, look towards better

Well-deserved is coming
It's only right, it has to be
That one day is very near
You simply have to believe

While you are waiting for more
Use that pain to move and soar

Love On Fire

Do what makes you happy, what makes you smile
Your heart, dreams and desires is all that's worth while

Once you stop worrying and start to focus on you
Others will look up and eventually notice you
Notice that you are special in everything you do
Notice that you have more than most, but great value

So wipe your eyes and lift up your head
It's much to do, great things ahead
Find your peace within, learn to love you
Know that no one controls your happiness, that's your job to do

Appreciate your pain, recognize its place
It had a reason for coming, so you could be better one day
It pushed you to do more, to let go and release
To later really enjoy and be in love with your peace

About the Author

Laverne Thomas is a 32-year old, wife and mother of two from Chicago. Born number 5 in a family of 9 children, she learned early on that family was important and something that she wanted for herself. After witnessing her parent's love for each other, the strength and support of a husband was always a desire to have. When she married her husband Daniel, her dreams were finally coming to life. Now, being together 8 years and married for 3 years, she has learned a few things about what it really means to be committed to love. Although having only been married for a few years, she quickly learned that married life was very different from the dating relationship.

Various dynamics within her personal, professional and spiritual life caused her to look at things very differently. She experienced pain, frustration and disappointment within different areas of her life from diverse situations. Instead of allowing those pressures of life to hinder her, she found her peace and strength through starting two businesses and writing this book. Her online inspirational store for children, Lil Angel Tees, encourages positivity in youth. Her event planning business, Blissful Dream Occasions, delivers happiness to others through making their events become more than they ever dreamed. Lastly her book, LOVE ON FIRE, gives helpful tips to men and women struggling with maintaining their love for each other in the mist of life changes. Through her businesses, writings and future projects, Laverne Thomas will definitely continue to be a support and encouragement to others while helping herself.

Love On Fire

www.ingramcontent.com/pod-product-compliance
Lightning Source LLC
Chambersburg PA
CBHW051718040426
42446CB00008B/947